MW01181022

DO YOU LOOK LIKE YOUR DOG?

by Gini Graham Scott, PhD

**CHANGEMAKERS PUBLISHING
AND WRITING**
6114 La Salle, #358 . Oakland, CA 94611
www.changemakerspublishingandwriting.com

Do You Look Like Your Dog?

Copyright © 2011 by Gini Graham Scott

Because of the dynamic nature of the Internet, any Web addresses or links contained in this book may have changed since publication and may no longer be valid.

ABOUT THE AUTHOR

GINI GRAHAM SCOTT, Ph.D., J.D., is a nationally known writer, consultant, speaker, and seminar/workshop leader, specializing in business and work relationships and in professional and personal development.

She has published over 50 books on diverse subjects, among them several books on social trends, including *The Very Next New Thing* and *Playing the Lying Game*. Her books on relationships in the workplace include *A Survival Guide for Working With Humans...Managing Employees From Hell...And Working With Bad Bosses*. Other books which deal with success and professional development include: *The Empowered Mind, How to Harness the Creative Force Within You; Mind Power: Picture Your Way to Success*; *The Innovative Edge;* and *Want It, See It, Get It!.* She has written several books on promoting and marketing your business, including: *Top Secrets for Doing Your Own PR* and *Top Secrets for Using LinkedIn to Promote Your Business or Yourself.*

She is founder and owner of Changemakers Publishing and Writing and Changemakers Productions, and has been a featured expert guest on hundreds of TV and radio shows, including Oprah and Good Morning America. She is the host of a weekly international talk radio talk, CHANGEMAKERS, on Blog Talk Radio featuring interviews and commentary on the latest developments in science, technology, business, and society. Her Websites for writing is www.changemakerspublishingandwriting.com and for books is www.ginigrahamscott.com.

She does workshops and consults on publishing books and promoting one's business or oneself through the social and traditional media. She has a service which sends out press releases to the media – the PR and Networking Connect at www.prandnetworkingconnection.com.

Scott additionally writes screenplays, mostly in the crime, legal thriller, and sci-fi genres, including RICH AND DEAD, COKE AND DIAMONDS, DEADLY AFFAIR, FLARE UP, DEAD NO MORE, THE NEW CHILD, NEW IDENTITY, and DELUSION. She produced, directed, wrote, cast, and sometimes directed over 40 short films and trailers, which are www.changemakersproductions.com and at www.youtube.com/changemakersprod.

As a game and toy designer, Scott has over two dozen games with major game companies, including Hasbro, Pressman, and Mag-Nif. Two new games were introduced by Briarpatch in 2007. She has written and demoed over 100 songs, which are featured at www.songworks.net.

She has a Ph.D. in Sociology from the University of California in Berkeley, a J.D. from the University of San Francisco Law School, and M.A.s in Anthropology; Mass Communications and Organizational/Consumer/Audience Behavior, and Popular Culture and Lifestyles from California State University, East Bay. She is getting an MS in Recreation and Tourism at Cal State.

She has been the producer and host of a talk show series, CHANGEMAKERS, featuring interviews on trends in science, technology, business, and society. Additional information is at www.changemakersradio.com.

Acknowledgments

First and foremost, I want to thank the many people who sent in their photos to the Do You Look Like Your Dog website or posed for photos at the dog shows and dog events I attended over the years. Without their contributions, this book—and the website that inspired it—would not have been possible.

Also, I wanted to extend my thanks to Peter Mason, who helped to set up the initial Do You Look Like Your Dog website about five years ago, when this book was still a proposal featuring photos from the first dog shows I attended in 1992 and 1993 at the Cow Palace near San Francisco.

Gini Graham Scott, Ph.D.

Introduction

We all know or have seen someone who looks noticeably like his or her canine companion. Maybe it's a jowly guy with a Bullmastiff, a high-style woman with a clipped French Poodle, Kathy Lee Gifford and her perky Bichon Frise, Paula Abdul with her spotted Chihuahua, or Homeland Security Director Tom Ridge with his husky Yellow Labs—or even George W. Bush and his English Springer Spaniel—whatever the combination, people resembling their dogs is a phenomenon that catches our attention and amuses everyone the world over. And it has certainly fascinated, intrigued, and entertained me for quite some time.

How It All Began

About 12,000 years ago, man domesticated the dog, a direct descendant of the wolf, an animal we had already developed a relationship with through hunting. Approximately 11,988 years later, I attended my first dog show in 1992. It was the Golden Gate Kennel Club Show, held at the Cow Palace near San Francisco, and it was, and is, one of the few benched shows in the United States. A benched show is one in which people are assigned to benches by the breed they are showing, which means you get an opportunity to see people grouped by the dogs they own. Going merely for diversion, I was struck by the number of people who had a remarkable resemblance to their show-dogs. So I returned that afternoon with my camera, and I found dozens of owners who were delighted to pose and show off with their pooches—many even commented on how often they were told they looked like their dogs, or observed that many people they knew looked like their canine friends. Fittingly, the only person who didn't want to be photographed was an angry-looking woman with a scowl to match the one on her Boston Terrier—as I have learned, people often resemble their dogs in demeanor and disposition as well as in physical appearance.

Thinking the subject might make a good book, I returned to the same show the following year and took another batch of photos of willing subjects. But when other events intervened and my life got busy with consulting, teaching, and other books, I put the project on hold. As other things filled up my life, the idea languished for about six years, until one day I was working on a consulting project for a client with a Web design company. While on the project I was introduced to the client's partner, Peter Mason, and his dashing Yellow Lab. I immediately noticed the resemblance, and in the course of our conversation I mentioned the photographs I had taken; together we came up with the idea to create a website, and so www.doyoulooklikeyour dog.com was born.

Slowly but surely in the year that followed, the site began to get more and more hits. People also started sending in photographs of their own, eager to join in the fun, and to show off their resemblances to their canines. It soon became clear that the site was striking a chord with dog lovers all over the world. Though Peter had to leave the website after two years to pursue his own projects, I continued it on my own, and as word of the site spread, I began getting dozens of submissions each month—even photographs from Canada, Italy, Romania, Israel, and New Zealand. Then, about a year ago, with over five hundred great photographs, I felt ready to take the idea to a publisher, and the response was overwhelming. You hold the result of that enthusiasm in your hands.

But *Why* Do People Look Like Their Dogs?

There is no definitive answer to this question, and that makes the phenomenon both so entertaining and so interesting. There have not been any conclusive scientific studies into this common link between people and their pets, but over the years of running the website and visiting dog shows, I've come up with a few theories on why so many dog owners tend to resemble their canine companions. I've even started doing some ethnographic research, based on in-depth interviews with owners at dog shows.

First and foremost, I think there is a fairly simple psychological explanation: just as people gravitate toward other people with whom they share an affinity, so it follows that people will often choose to own pets with whom they feel some kind of connection. Sometimes the choice is very conscious and deliberate, sometimes subconscious, but often people naturally seek out pets who bear some resemblance to themselves, since physical likeness breeds a natural sense of familiarity. It's the same reason that people tend to look like their mates.

Then, too, there is the theory that people can *grow* to look like their canine pals. Just as we often observe couples growing closer in physical likeness over the years they spend together, many people will develop stronger and stronger resemblances to their pets as they live together, developing a stronger and closer relationship. This is especially true today, when people commonly think of their pets as family members. Since a person's pet is in many ways an extension of him- or herself, a dog owner's interests and lifestyle will often influence the way both the dog and owner look. For example, someone very interested in appearance might spend a lot of time grooming his or her furry friend, and both will have a similarly stylish look—many times they will have the same hairstyle, or people will dress their pets in clothes to match their own. Someone more interested in sports and the great outdoors might have a more muscular, rugged-looking pet, and that person may be more physically fit and muscular, too.

Who Looks Like Their Dog the Most, and How?

Intriguingly, certain breeds tend to look like their owners more than others. Far and away the breed with the highest incidence of resemblance in the submissions I have received is the Golden Retriever. After that, I found Collies (particularly the Rough and the Bearded breeds), Irish Wolfhounds, Lhasa Apsos, and Poodles to be breeds where people felt a great physical likeness to themselves.

It is also interesting to note the variety of ways in which people can look like their tail-wagging counterparts. One of the first things you may notice is similar hair style, length, or color, such as the women who have long flowing hair like their Collies, or the bald man who has a hairless Greyhound.

Other characteristics that owners and dogs share are facial features and expressions. A woman with a Basset Hound might have the same sad, droopy look, while a man with a Rottweiler or a Bulldog might have tough, rugged features. People will often resemble their dogs in body type, too. Often you will see a long, lean Greyhound with an owner who has a similar thin build, or a stocky and muscular man or woman with a Bullmastiff or Saint Bernard.

So, do you look like your dog? Or do you know friends, neighbors, or relatives who look like theirs? As

you look at the pictures in this book, you will see that
people can look like their dogs in many different ways,
and there are many possible reasons why they do. But
whatever the reason, it is a phenomenon that cannot be
denied. Love it, laugh at it, celebrate it, marvel at it—
above all, enjoy it.

How Do I Look Like Thee?

Let Me Count the Ways . . .

It's the Hair:

The short and sheared look.

Julie David of Boca Raton, Florida, and Princess Tierra
Elizabeth, a Hairless Chinese Crested.

2   Do You Look Like Your Dog?

Matching white locks.

Bruce Tripp of Oakland, California, with his Maltese, Angel.

The short . . .

Kristin Kuamstrom of Rancho Murietta, California, with
Tawny Mist Secret Keeper, a Silky Terrier.

... and long of it.

Anne Ellefsen of San Jose, California, with Olav,
a Bearded Collie Cross.

Big hair.

Cindy Weiner of Turlock, California, with Cody and Cruiser, her
Rough Collies. She was one of my first discoveries.

Mary Fanti of Ontario, Canada, with Sofie, her Pomeranian.

Short hair.

Suzanne McCombs of Anderson, California, with Teagan,
an Irish Wolfhound.

From golden locks to silky blondes . . .

Jennifer Smith of Antioch, California, with Ginger,
a Golden Retriever.

Wendy McPhillips of Redwood City, California, with Lola,
a Golden Retriever.

Kathy Coon of San Jose, California, with Rowdy, a Shetland
Sheepdog (Sheltie). Another early find.

Shari Arata of San Jose, California, with Holly, a very Silky Terrier.

Hard to tell whether this husband and wife look more like their dogs or each other.

James Mitchell of Fair Oaks, California, with Lancelot, a Bichon Frise.

Kay Mitchell with Lucky, their other Bichon Frise.

Do You Look Like Your Dog?

Blondes have more fun.

Sherri Regalbuto of Mission Viejo, California, with Luke,
an apricot-colored Poodle.

But brunettes don't do so badly.

Lorna Pumphrey of Stockton, California, with Kassie,
an Irish Water Spaniel.

Barbara D. Beebe of Redwood City, California, with Captain and
Tillie, a brace of Standard Poodles. Looks like a long,
bad hair day for everyone.

Sheri Holihan of Yuba City, California,
with Chila Karis de Media Noche, a Havanese.

The ears—and hair—have it.

Terry Kelso of Novato, California, with Sadie,
a Cocker Spaniel.

Hair today ...

Joanne Weber of Stuart, Florida, with Daisy,
an English Springer Spaniel.

Rosey Gilbertson of Rochester, Minnesota, with Hawkeye,
an English Springer Spaniel.

Marcia O'Kane of Castro Valley, California,
with her Cocker Spaniel, Roxy.

The gang's all hair . . .

Linda Masys of San Diego, California,
with Muffy, a Shih Tzu.

Rachel Meyer of Santa Cruz, California,
with Journey and Sienna, Irish Setters.

Robi Anderson, a professional animal handler from Rancho Mirage, California, with Bart, a Jack Russell Terrier and an aspiring performer.

Clip job.

Clyde Schauer of Burlingame, California, with Crystal,
a Soft Coated Wheaten Terrier.

Double your pleasure . . .

Polly Armstrong of Berkeley, California, with Franklin
and Theodore, two Bichon Frises.

... double your fun.

Lynne Rosebrock of Mariposa, California, with Donovan and Rosie,
a couple of Irish Wolfhounds.

The next star and understudy in
AMADEUS.

Paul L. Keevil of Surrey, England, with Crosby,
a Dandie Dinmont Terrier.

Bearded Wonders

Just a little off the bottom, please.

Max Spurlock of Kensington, California, with King's Mountain
Westminster Abby, a Dandie Dinmont Terrier.

Sleepy time terrier.

Harold Julander of Santa Rosa, California,
with Farside, his Border Terrier.

Peek-a-boo!

Steve Pyne of Bloomington, Illinois, with Tucker,
a Peekapoo (Pekinese-Poodle cross).

A meeting of the Executive Board.

Gary Barnett of Minden, New Hampshire, with Mae
and Linny, his (sleeping) Irish Wolfhounds.

Ho! Ho! Ho!

Bob Lewis of Auckland, New Zealand, with Sam,
a Poodle (Reindeer?) cross.

A set of well-clipped mustaches.

Lou Patrick of Smithtown, Pennsylvania,
with Mariah Marie, a Lhasa Apso.

Face to Face

Cheek to cheek . . .

Candice Morgan of San Diego, California, with Chloe,
a Yorkshire Terrier (Yorkie, for short).

Monique Groom of British Columbia, Canada,
with Chatchka, a Chihuahua.

Tom Ford of Brusly, Louisiana, with Missy, his Labrador Retriever.

Susan Lane of Denver, Colorado, with Bailey Molson Riley,
a Yellow Labrador puppy.

Face-off.

Stacey Borrman of Redwood City, California,
with Candi, her Akita.

Long and lean . . .

Nichole Torre of Santa Rosa, California, with
Sugar Ray, her Doberman.

Jackie Lakin of Medford, Oregon,
with Sweet William, an Italian Greyhound.

Do You Look Like Your Dog?

Susan Sonza of Santa Rosa, California, with Anna,
a Miniature Pinscher.

All ears.

Ken Piercy of Durham, California, with Gadget, a French Bulldog.

Love that camera!

Judith Markwardt of Milwaukee, Wisconsin, with Taz, her Pomeranian.

Size Does Matter

Big guys, big dogs.

Dave Briggs of Redwood City, California, and Chris Kushner
of Folsom, California, with their Bullmastiffs,
Grainne and Bella, respectively.

Lance Griffin of Griffin, Georgia, with Zoe, his French Mastiff.

Big dogs, big laughs . . . What's so funny?

Margo Lauritsea of Pleasanton, California, with Ripley and Molly,
a pair of English Mastiffs.

In the thick of things.

Linda Hunter of Pleasanton, California,
with Willow, a Saint Bernard.

May to December

For some, the resemblance starts early.

Hannah Mary Cruger of Middle Island, New York,
with Benjamin, her Spaniel.

Brittney Bundy of Oakland, California, with Prince, her Maltese.

Merick Ethan Wild of Cambridge, Ohio, with Rudy, a Long
Haired Miniature Dachshund.

For others, it lasts a lifetime.

Jack Taylor of San Diego, California, with Mike, a Lhasa Apso.

Tough Dogs Don't Dance

But he's really a pussycat at heart.

Clyde Shigeta of Inglewood, California, with Green, a mixed breed.

You talkin' to me?

Gene Settel of Carlisle, Pennsylvania, with Lydia, a Bullmastiff.
He calls this picture "Jowls."

Whaddya bench?

Michael Wells of Montgomery Creek, California,
with Zac, a Bullmastiff.

Biker guys with biker dogs.

Mark Shaffer of San Diego, California, with Bandit, a Boston Terrier.

Rusty Thorsgard of Imperial Beach, California,
with T. J., his Chihuahua.

Born to be wild.

Jesse Lane of Oakland, California, and the website
dogsonbikes.com, with Houdini, a Schipperke.

Don't Toy with Me

Girls love their toys . . .

April Martin of Oakley, California, with Buster Brown,
a Long Coat Chihuahua.

Carolyn Latorre of Sonora, California, with
Topper, a Pomeranian.

. . . and so do boys!

Ray Schulte of British Columbia, Canada, with Gidget,
a.k.a. Bumblebee, a Chihuahua.

Man's Best Friend

Bobby's the one with the glasses.

Bobby Sher of Toronto, Canada, with Ricky, a Schnauzer.

Good Boy Blue's the one without the glasses.

Mike McKenzie of Tacoma, Washington, with Good Boy Blue, a
Catahoula Leopard Dog. He plays a mean game of Frisbee.

Grim and grimmer.

J. Michael Bell of Lodi, California, with
Street Legal, his Bullmastiff.

ME? Why don't YOU fetch for once?

Paul Keasberry of San Rafael, California, with
Albert, a Rottweiler.

Wassup?

Mike Redmon of Jefferson, Ohio, with Butch, his aptly named English
Bulldog. Not only do they look alike, but they snore alike too.

A close shave.

Brad Manges of Pittsburgh, Pennsylvania, with Kenya, a Greyhound.

Mush, mush!

J. Glen Palmer of Concord, California, with Diesel,
an Alaskan Malamute.

And Woman's

Best Friend, Too . . .

Sitting pretty.

Katherine Field of New Vineyard, Maine, with Bugaboo,
a Chesapeake Bay Retriever.

Things are looking up.

Dee Dee Murry of Centralia, Washington, with Hallie, her Miniature
Longhaired Dachshund, both looking thoughtful.

Pugnacious?

Mary Ortez of Tracy, California, with J. J.,
the Pug with the furrowed brow.

White lightning . . .

Cindy Hopkins of Orangevale, California,
with Honey, a Samoyed.

Smile and Your Dog
Smiles with You

Say CHEESE!

Celia Sawyer of Torrance, California, with Aynsley,
a (very) Bearded Collie.

Kathy Plante of Quebec, Canada, with
Oscar, a Labrador Retriever.

Cindy Sturges of Dayton, Nevada, with Winston, a Labrador Retriever.

Shaun Helmey of Roswell, Georgia, with
Keena, his Siberian Husky.

Rough love.

Bonnie Kay Grindle of Santa Clara, California, hugging
her one and only MacDuff, a Rough Collie.

White knights.

Wilna Coulter of San Carlos, California, with Whitecliff's Alexis
and a Samoyed friend.

No bull!

Rob Grankni of Sunnyvale, California, with
Twister, a Bull Terrier.

Anna Virina of Ashdod, Israel, with Gosha, a mixed
breed she found on the street.

Or DONT say cheese.

Susan Kelman of Richmond, California, with Jada, a Bulldog.

Hold that pose.

Stewart Mundy of Brentwood, California, with Jason,
a Chinese Shar-Pei.

Dressed for Success

Ready for Everest.

Jacquelyn Briley of Detroit, Michigan, with Buddy and
Bamm Bamm, her two Cairn Terriers.

In the hood.

Tina Bornheimer of Newark, New York, with Kody Jacob, a Labrador
Retriever. In his spare time, Kody Jacob likes to shake hands
(or paws), and he also enjoys break-dancing.

Bummed out.

Lynda Long of Winnipeg, Canada, with Colby, a Border
Collie/Golden Retriever mix.

Do you look like your dog? I do.

Sheila H. Curtis of Varnville, South Carolina, with Daisy,
a Miniature Pinscher.

Checkmate.

Katie Finn of Los Angeles, California, with Gypsy,
a rescued Chihuahua mix.

Putting on the dog. Literally.

Linda Crabill of San Jose, California, with Kelly, a Lhasa
Apso of international dog show acclaim.

Jackie Lockwood of Ripon, California, with Murphy,
a West Highland White Terrier.

Don Avila of Ducor, California, with Booda, his Chow Chow.

It's All About Knowing
How to Accessorize . . .

Great shades!

Chrystal Anne Grondin of Olathe, Kansas, with Precious Lady
Princess, a very hip Golden Retriever.

Tennis, anyone?

Beth Goldstein of Laguna Beach, California, with
Laguna Mirage, an Airedale Terrier.

Minnie Mouseketeers.

Joan Luna of Beavercreek, Oregon, with Scarlett, a Samoyed.

Picture perfect.

Tiffany Anne Pippin of Billings, Montana, with Bridgett,
a Yorkshire Terrier.

Supermodels.

Hannah Belle Crowley of Salem, Massachusetts, with
George, a dashing Pomeranian.

Alexandra Blantyre of Salt Lake City, Utah,
with Shammy, a Tibetan Spaniel.

SPOT the Resemblance— 101 Minus 98 Dalmatians

A great spot for sleeping.

Les and Kevin Casazza of Concord, California,
taking a nap with Jewel, a Dalmatian.

Matching coats.

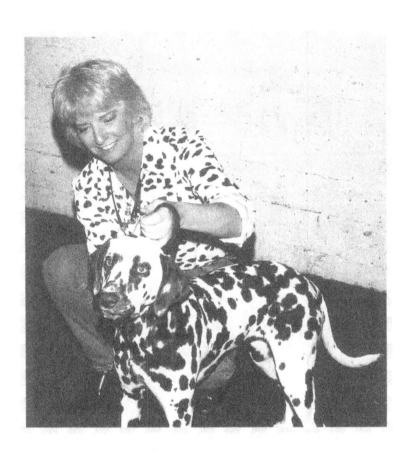

Teresa Utterback of Shingle Springs, California, with Domino,
a Dalmatian.

Winner by a nose.

Lynn Christian of Ames, Iowa, going incognito
with Agate, a Dalmatian.

Hail and farewell!

Michelle Rosenfeld of New York, New York, with Barbie,
a Chinese Shar-Pei.

Photographic Credits

NOTE: *Except where stated below, all photos were taken by the author.*

page 2:   Julie David and Princess Tierra Elizabeth, photograph by Glamour Shots

page 3:   Bruce Tripp and Angel, photograph by Cleo Brown

page 5:   Anne Ellefsen and Olav, photograph by Cleo Brown

page 7:   Mary Fanti and Sofie, photograph by Nicole Fanti

page 12:   Shari Arata and Holly, photograph by Shirley Baker

page 15:   Sherri Regalbuto and Luke, photograph by Steve Regalbuto

page 20:   Joanne Weber and Daisy, photograph by Cathy D. Baker

page 21:   Rosey Gilbertson and Hawkeye, photograph by Proex, Apache Mall

page 22:   Marcia O'Kane and Roxy, photograph by Cleo Brown

page 23:   Linda Masys and Muffy, photograph by Linda Masys

page 25:   Robi Anderson and Bart, photograph by Photo Galleria

page 29:   Paul L. Keevil and Crosby, photograph by Tim Rose (for "Dogs Today")

page 34:   Steve Pyne and Tucker, photograph by Kathleen O'Grady-Pyne

page 36:   Bob Lewis and Sam, photograph by Tracy Lewis

✳

OTHER BOOKS BY THE AUTHOR

Here are other books on achieving success and promoting yourself or your business by the author:

- *WANT IT, SEE IT, GET IT! VISUALIZE YOUR WAY TO SUCCESS*
- *USING LINKEDIN TO PROMOTE YOUR BUSINESS OR YOURSELF*
- *THE COMPLETE GUIDE TO DOING YOUR OWN PR*
- *30 DAYS TO A MORE POWERFUL MEMORY*
- *ENJOY: 101 LITTLE THINGS TO ADD FUN TO YOUR WORK EVERYDAY*
- *RESOLVING CONFLICT*
- *A SURVIVAL GUIDE FOR WORKING WITH HUMANS*
- *A SURVIVAL GUIDE FOR WORKING WITH BAD BOSSES*
- *A SURVIVAL GUIDE TO MANAGING EMPLOYEES FROM HELL*

AUTHOR CONTACT INFORMATION

Here's how to contact the author for information about other books and about speaking for your organization or putting on workshops and seminars for your organization:

Gini Graham Scott, PhD
Director
Changemakers Publishing and Writing
6114 La Salle, #358
Oakland, CA 94611
(510) 339-1625
changemakers@pacbell.net
www.changemakerspublishingandwriting.com
www.changemakersproductions.com

CPSIA information can be obtained
at www.ICGtesting.com
Printed in the USA
BVHW041940111218
535365BV00017B/255/P